The FJH Young Beginner Guitar

T0012297

COMPILED AND
ARRANGED BY
PHILIP GROEBER
AND DAVID HOGE

Production: Frank J. Hackinson

Production Coordinator: Philip Groeber

Cover Design/Illustrations: Gwen Terpstra

Interior Illustration Layout: Andi Whitmer

Cover Photo: courtesy of C.F. Martin Guitar & Co. Inc., Nazareth, PA

Engraving: Tempo Music Press, Inc.

Printer: Tempo Music Press, Inc.

ISBN-13: 978-1-61928-174-5

A Note to the Teacher

The FJH Young Beginner Guitar Method is a carefully graded course designed to instruct the modern guitarist to be proficient in solo playing, chord accompaniment, and chord-melody style. Solid musicianship skills are developed by exposing the student to the many styles typically encountered in today's musical world.

The series consists of five books for each level:
- Lesson
- Theory Activity
- Performance
- Exploring Chords
- Christmas

This book is a perfect companion to **The FJH Young Beginner Guitar Method Book 1**. The melodies for all of the Christmas songs use notes learned in **Lesson Book 1** and the chords use only three or four strings, similar to the chords learned in **Exploring Chords Book 1**. Any rhythm a student is not familiar with can be taught by rote.

The FJH Young Beginner Christmas Book 1 includes the following features:

- A pre-reading selection allows the student to play music by reading fret numbers only, as introduced in the Lesson Book 1.

- The student learns basic notes (natural notes in **first position** on strings one, two, and three) and rhythms (whole, dotted half, half, and quarter notes), making the **The FJH Young Beginner Guitar Method** an ideal starting point for elementary guitarists of all ages.

- Left-hand finger numbers are indicated at the entry of each new note in every song.

- This book is equally adaptable to pick-style or classical technique.

- Chord names with EZ Play Frames are included throughout the book to provide an opportunity for the beginning guitarist to strum chord accompaniment. The teacher or another guitarist can strum the chord voicings that are shown on page 28. A pianist may also accompany by using the chord names.

- The songs and pieces in this book are suitable for public performance.

G1065

Contents

Jingle Bells

James Pierpont

Student solo on the first string

E

4 4 4 | 4 4 4 | 4 7 0 2 | 4

Jin - gle bells, jin - gle bells, jin - gle all the way;

5

A   **E**   **F♯7**   **B7**

5 5 5 5 | 5 4 4 4 4 | 4 2 2 4 | 2 7

Oh, what fun it is to ride in a one - horse o - pen sleigh._____

 The large numbers represent the frets to be played on the first string. The small numbers (above the large numbers) represent the left-hand finger numbers.

Melody (in notation)

4

G1065

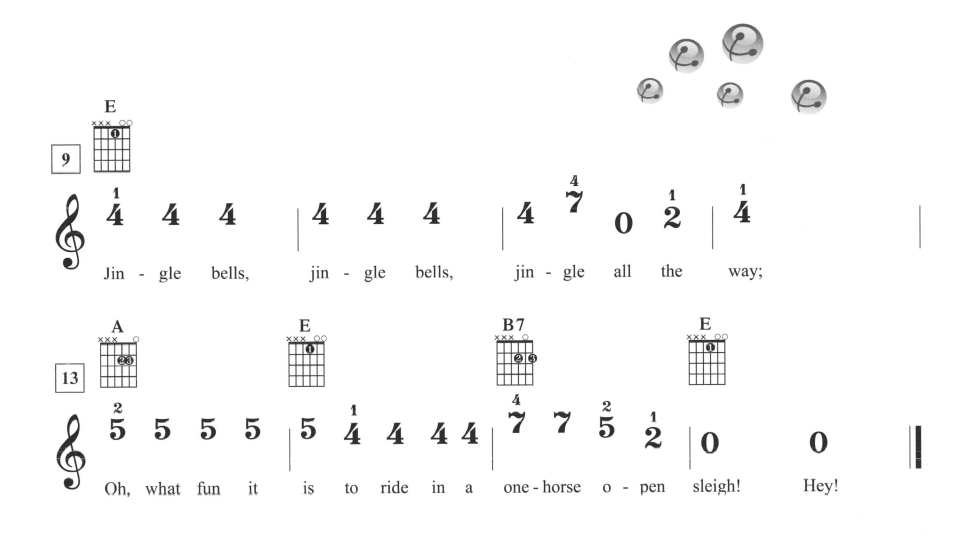

Jolly Old Saint Nicholas

Traditional

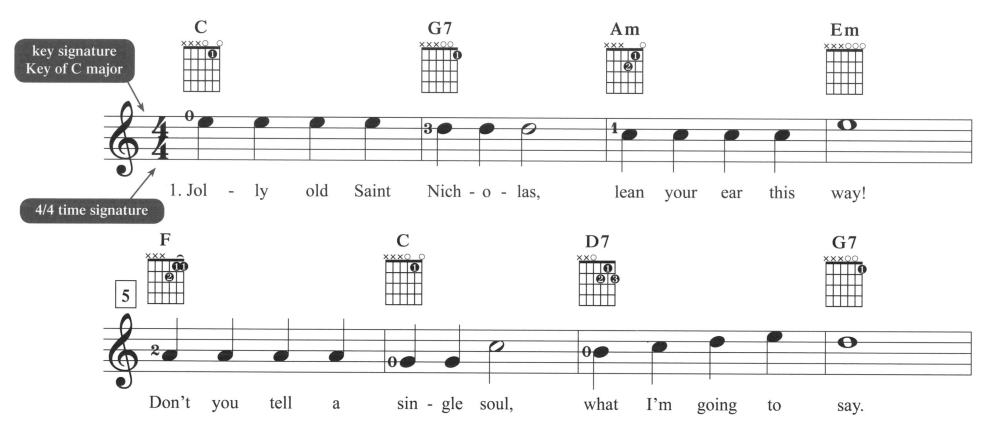

The key signature for a song in the Key of C major has no sharps or flats.

The small numbers next to the noteheads indicated the correct left-hand fingers to use when you play the notes. Using the correct finger will help you play more accurately.

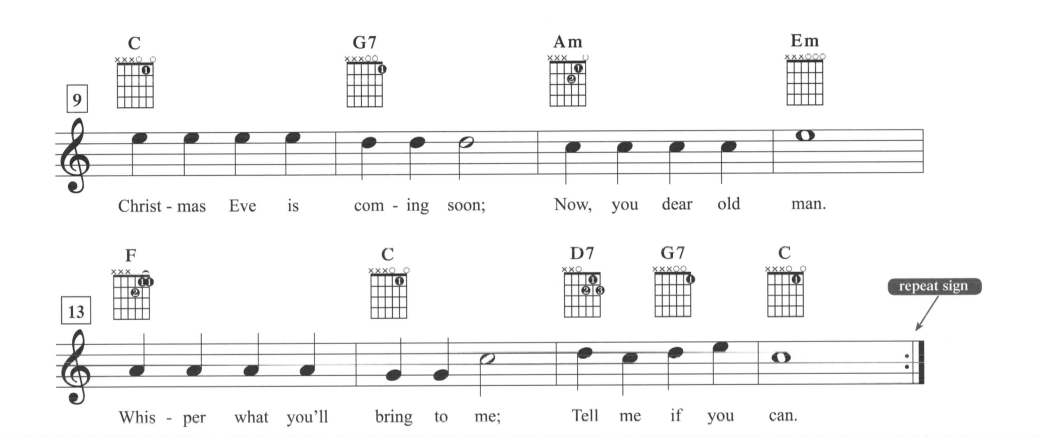

C   **G7**   **Am**   **Em**

9

Christ - mas Eve is com - ing soon; Now, you dear old man.

F   **C**   **D7**   **G7**   **C**

13

repeat sign

Whis - per what you'll bring to me; Tell me if you can.

Additional Lyrics

2. When the clock is striking twelve, when I'm fast asleep.
   Down the chimney broad and black, with your pack you'll creep.
   All the stockings you will find, hanging in a row.
   Mine will be the shortest one, you'll be sure to know.

Away in a Manger

Words: Traditional

Music by J. E. Spillman

Songs with a time signature of 3/4 have three beats per measure. *Away in a Manger* uses a pick-up note at the very beginning of the song starting on beat three.

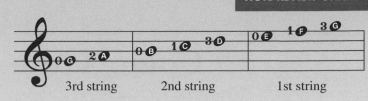

3rd string   2nd string   1st string

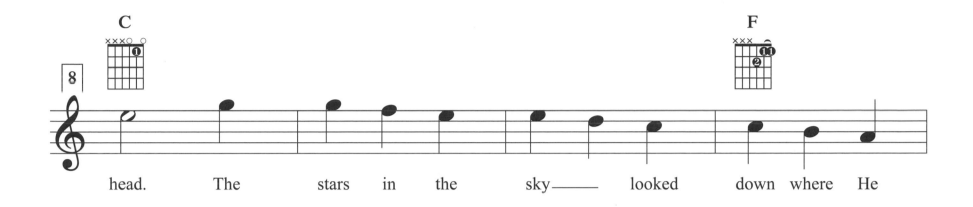

head.   The   stars   in   the   sky——   looked   down   where   He

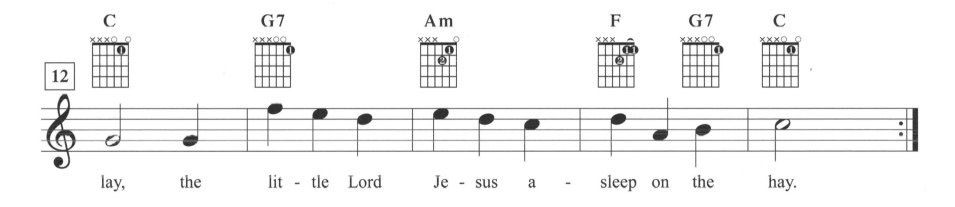

lay,   the   lit - tle   Lord   Je - sus   a - sleep   on   the   hay.

Additional Lyrics

2. The cattle are lowing, the Baby awakes,
   but little Lord Jesus, no crying He makes.
   I love Thee, Lord Jesus, look down from the sky,
   and stay by my bedside 'til morning is nigh.

3. Be near me, Lord Jesus, I ask Thee to stay,
   close by me for ever and love me, I pray.
   Bless all the dear children in Thy tender care,
   and take us to Heaven to live with Thee there.

O Come, Little Children

Words by Christoph von Schmid

Music by Johann A. P. Schulz

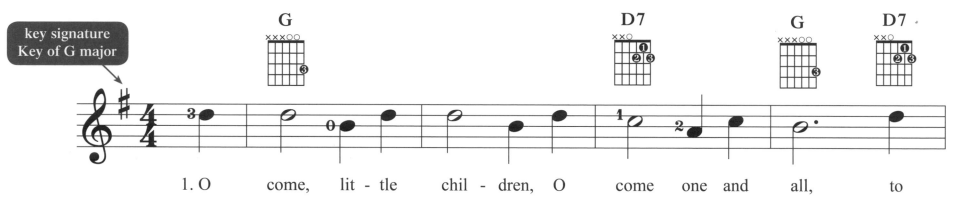

1. O come, lit-tle chil-dren, O come one and all, to

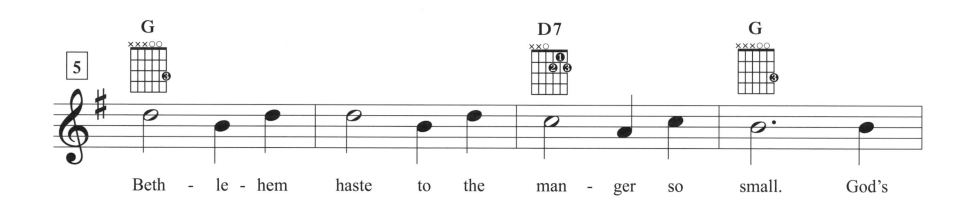

Beth-le-hem haste to the man-ger so small. God's

MUSIC MASTER The key signature of one sharp indicates that this song is in the Key of G major. This means that ALL of the F notes will be played as sharps (one fret higher). However, *O Come Little, Children* does not have any F notes in the entire song! Even so, the song is still in the Key of G major.

G1065

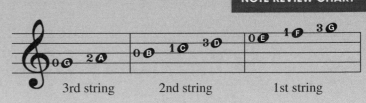

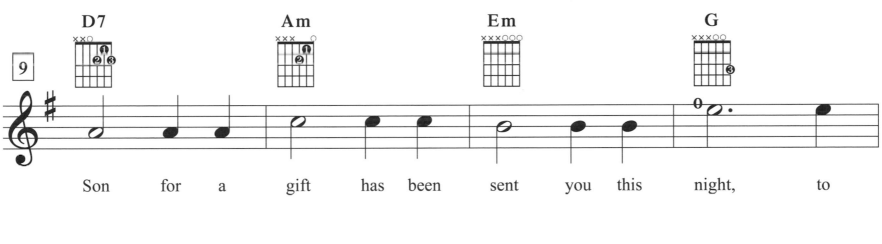

Son for a gift has been sent you this night, to

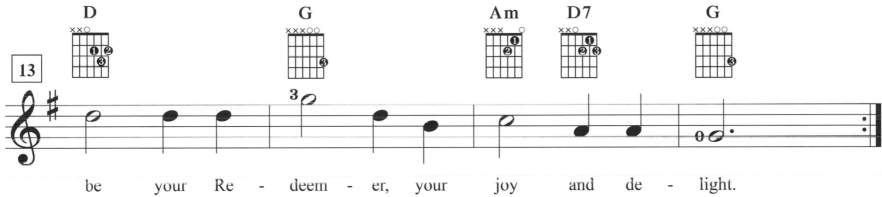

be your Re - deem - er, your joy and de - light.

Additional Lyrics

2. He's born in a stable for you and for me,
draw near by the bright gleaming starlight to see.
In swaddling clothes lying so meek and so mild,
and purer than angels the heavenly Child.

3. See Mary and Joseph, will love beaming eyes,
are gazing upon the rude bed where He lies.
The shepherds are kneeling, with hearts full of love,
while angels sing loud hallelujahs above.

Christmas Bells
(Round)

Traditional

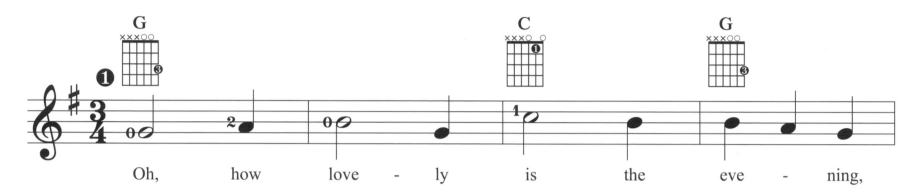

Oh, how love - ly is the eve - ning,

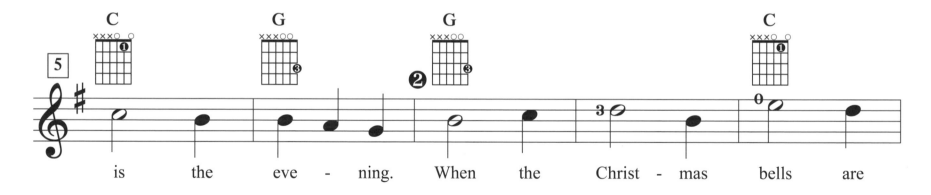

is the eve - ning. When the Christ - mas bells are

MUSIC MASTER

Christmas Bells is written in a musical style called a round. To perform this song as a round, you need at least two players; but three is better. A fourth player could strum the chords.

Player 1 begins as usual at the first measure. Player 2 begins at the first measure as Player 1 gets to ❷. Player 3 begins from the first measure as Player 1 gets to ❸.

Play as long as you wish. If Player 3 ends up playing the last six measures alone, then everything worked out perfectly!

G1065

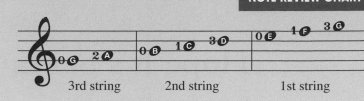

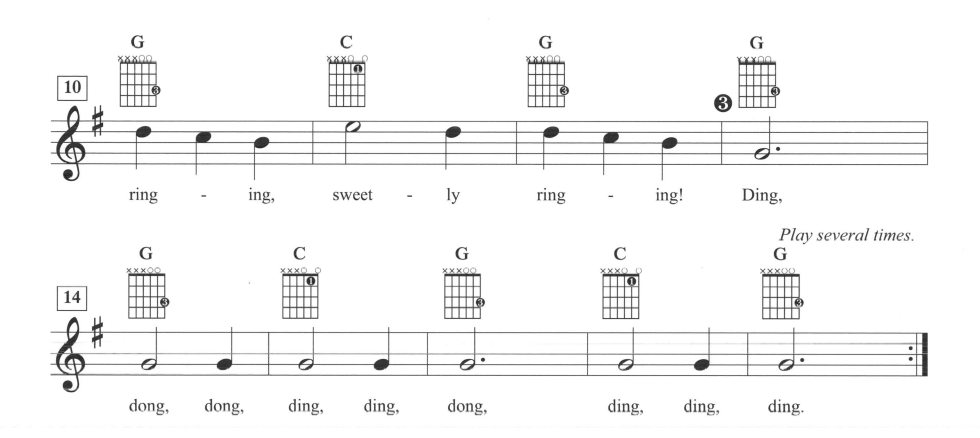

ring - ing, sweet - ly ring - ing! Ding,

Play several times.

dong, dong, ding, ding, dong, ding, ding, ding.

Below is a list of other familiar rounds that you will want to play.

Dona Nobis Pacem
Frére Jacques (Are You Sleeping?)
Hey, Ho, Nobody Home
Oh, How Lovely is the Evening
Row, Row, Row Your Boat
Three Blind Mice

Hope It's Santa

Philip Groeber

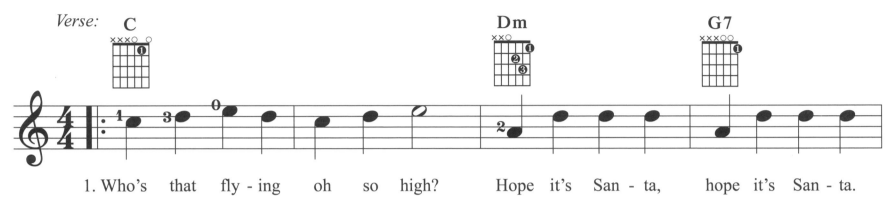

Verse:

1. Who's that fly - ing oh so high? Hope it's San - ta, hope it's San - ta.
2. Who's that in a suit of red? Hope it's San - ta, hope it's San - ta.

accent mark

Ti - ny rein - deer in the sky. We all hope it's San - ta Claus!
Lean - ing on his rein - deer sled. We all hope it's San - ta Claus!

Santa left one note value out in *Hope It's Santa*. Can you draw this note on his hat? Which note is it? *quarter note   half note   dotted half note   whole note*

14   G106

G106

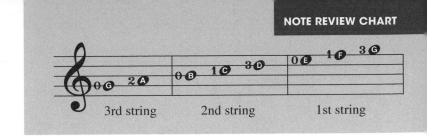

3rd string | 2nd string | 1st string

Chorus:

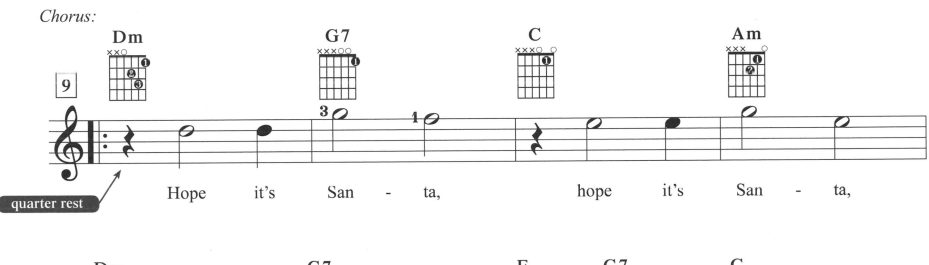

9

Dm   G7   C   Am

quarter rest

Hope   it's   San - ta,   hope   it's   San - ta,

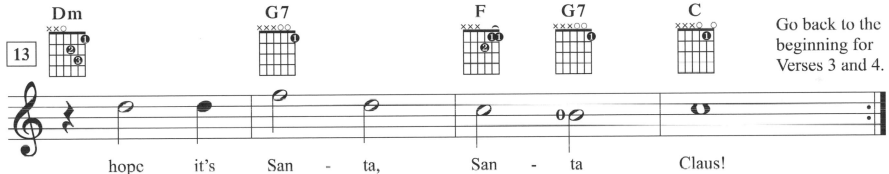

13

Dm   G7   F   G7   C

Go back to the beginning for Verses 3 and 4.

hope   it's   San - ta,   San - ta   Claus!

Additional Lyrics

3. Who's that laughing, "Ho, Ho, Ho?" Hope it's Santa, hope it's Santa.
   Sounds like someone that we know, we all hope it's Santa Claus!
4. Who's that kneeling by our tree? Hope it's Santa, hope it's Santa.
   Sacks of toys for you and me, we all hope it's Santa Claus!

We Three Kings of Orient Are

John H. Hopkins

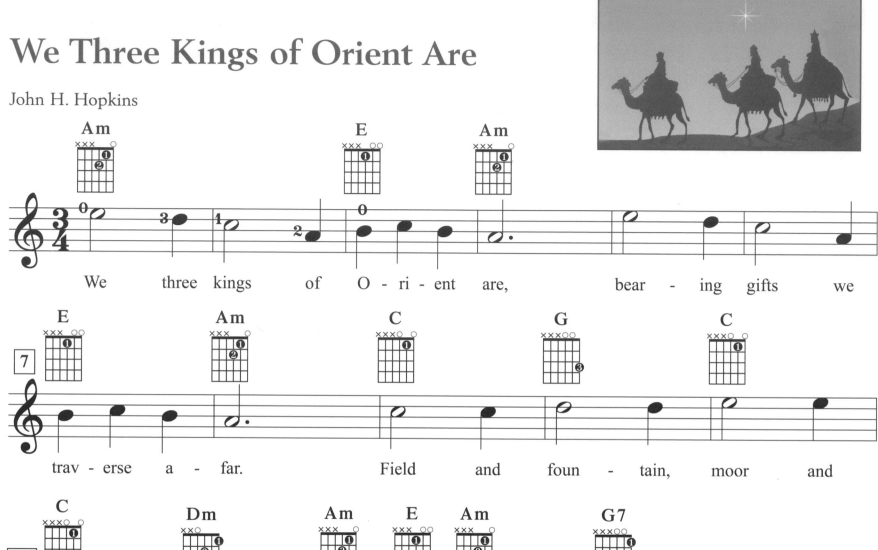

We three kings of O - ri - ent are, bear - ing gifts we

trav - erse a - far. Field and foun - tain, moor and

moun - tain, fol - low - ing yon - der star. Oh.

Here is a list of the three kings and the gifts that they presented to the Magi:
Balthazar (myrrh), Gaspar (gold), Melchior (frankincense).

G1065

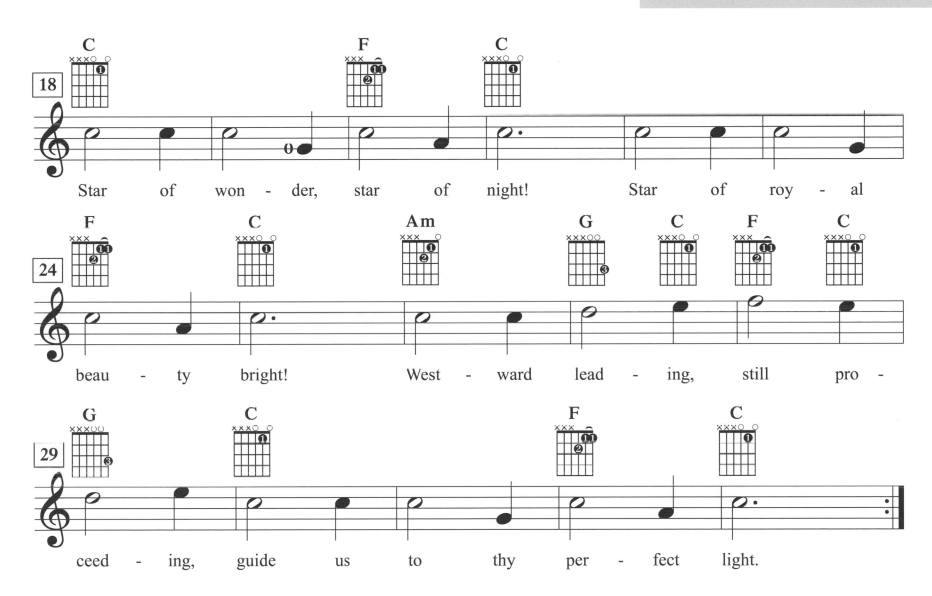

Additional Lyrics

2. Born a king on Bethlehem's plain, gold I bring to crown Him again.
King forever, ceasing never, over us all to reign. Oh.

Christmas Music Activities

A Cheery Christmas Crossword

Complete this crossword puzzle by using words from the song titles!
Every song title is included.

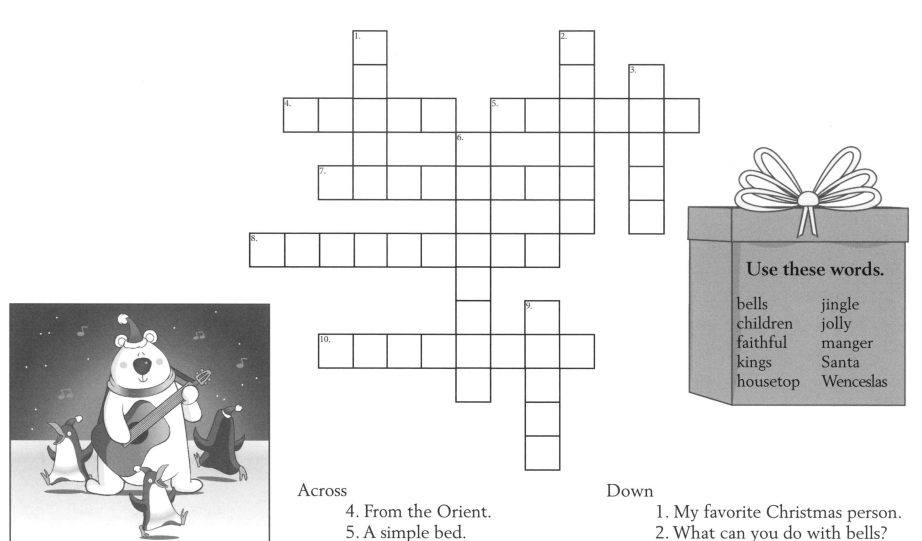

Use these words.

bells	jingle
children	jolly
faithful	manger
kings	Santa
housetop	Wenceslas

Across

4. From the Orient.
5. A simple bed.
7. O come all ye _____
8. He was a good king.
10. Reindeer often walk here.

Down

1. My favorite Christmas person.
2. What can you do with bells?
3. You can jingle these.
6. Wonderful little people.
9. Very happy.

Music Matching

Draw a line from each Christmas gift to the music term or symbol that best describes it.

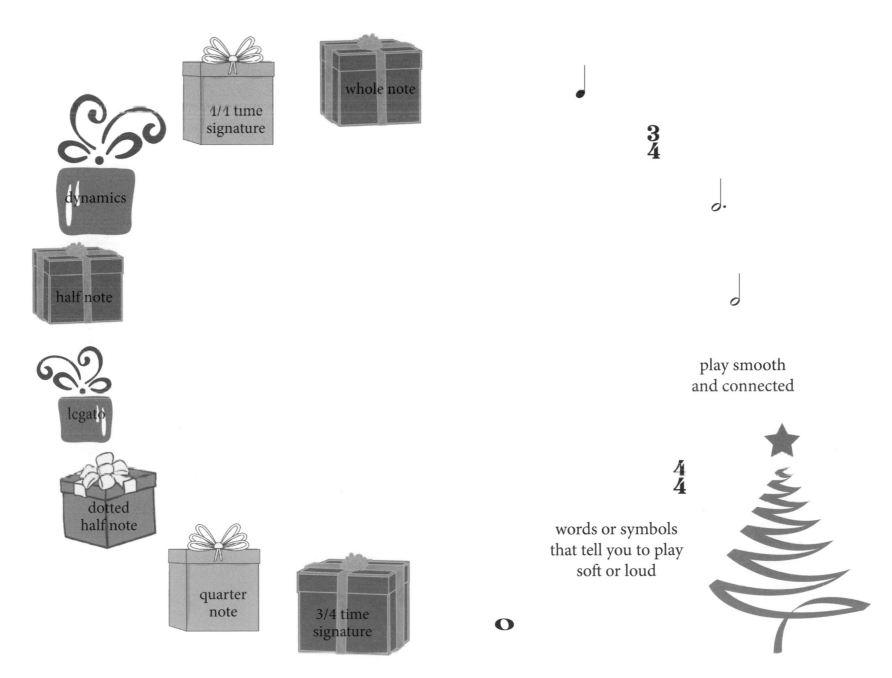

- 4/4 time signature
- whole note
- dynamics
- half note
- legato
- dotted half note
- quarter note
- 3/4 time signature

- ♩
- **3/4**
- ♩.
- ♩
- play smooth and connected
- **4/4**
- words or symbols that tell you to play soft or loud
- 𝅝

O Come, All Ye Faithful

Adeste Fideles

English lyrics by Frederick Oakeley
Music by John F. Wade

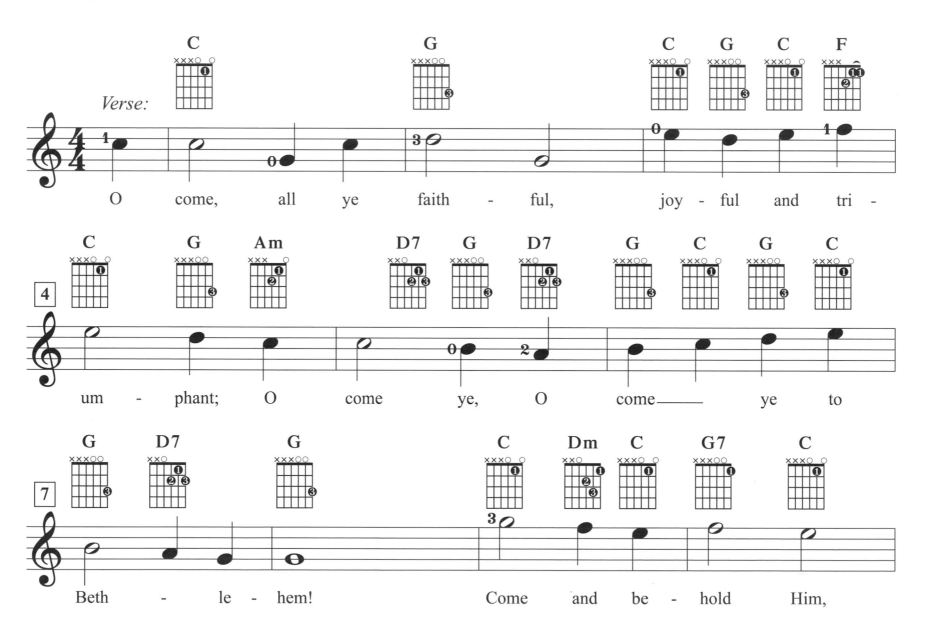

O come, all ye faith - ful, joy - ful and tri -

um - phant; O come ye, O come_____ ye to

Beth - le - hem! Come and be - hold Him,

G1065

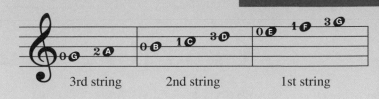

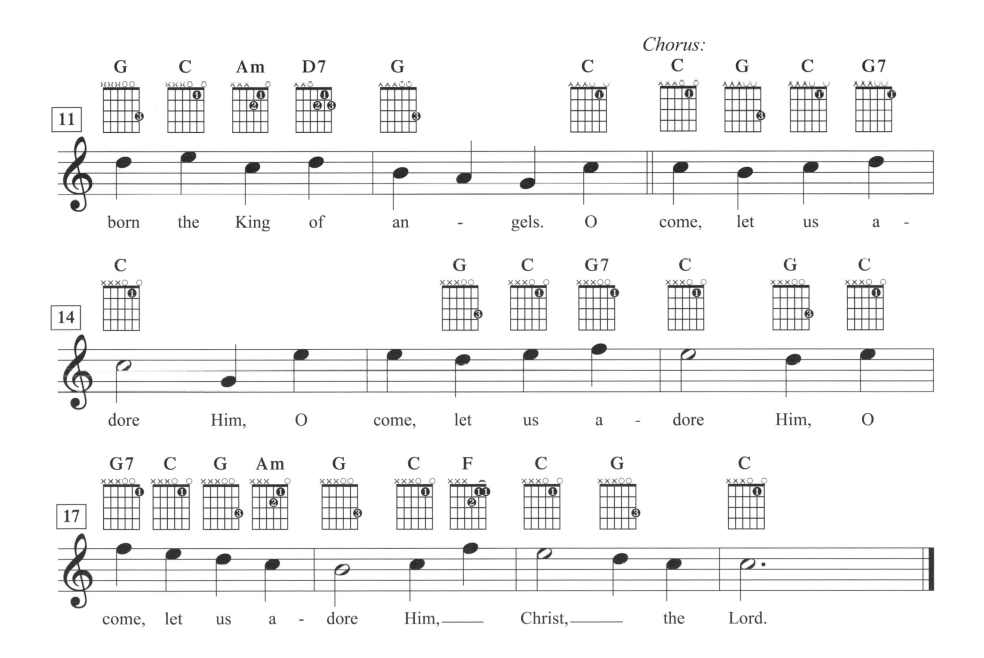

Good King Wenceslas

Words by John Mason Neale
Music: Traditional

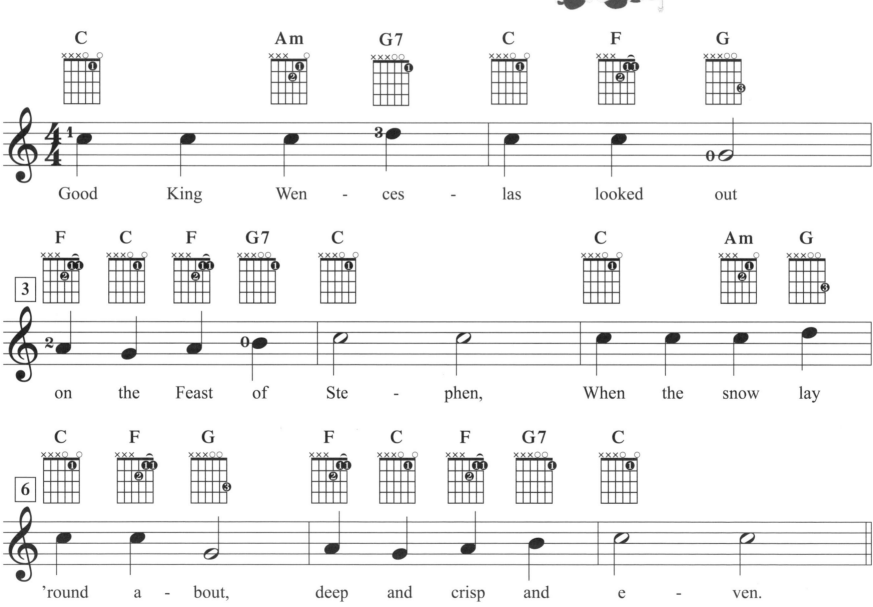

♩ = 84

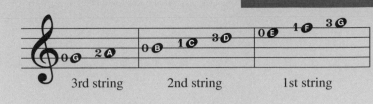

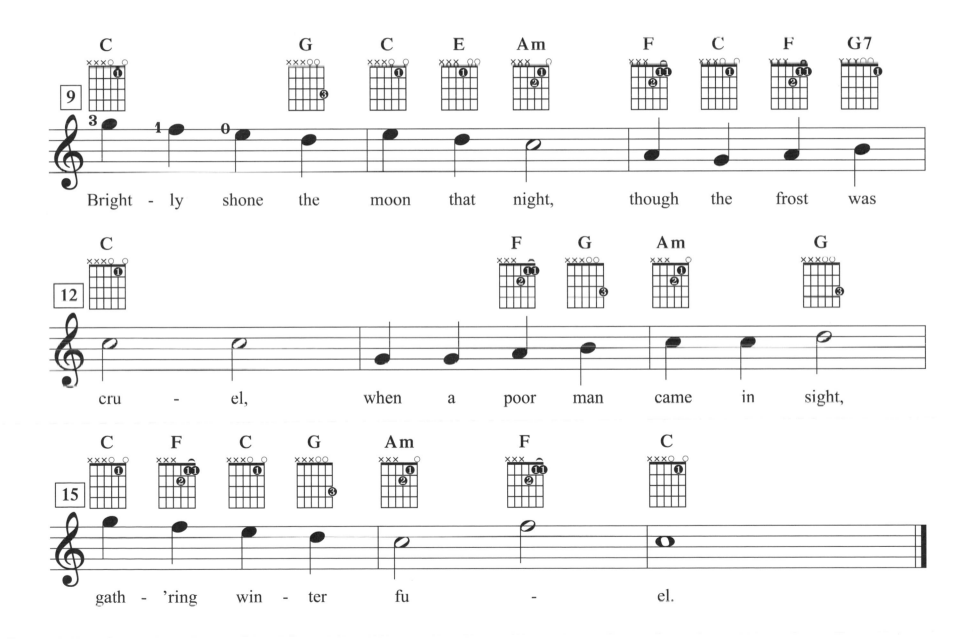

Bright - ly shone the moon that night, though the frost was

cru - el, when a poor man came in sight,

gath - 'ring win - ter fu - el.

Up On the Housetop

Benjamin R. Hanby

| G | Bm | Em | G7 | C |

Up on the house - top rein - deer pause, out jumps

| G | Am | D7 | G | Bm |

good old San - ta Claus. Down through the chim-ney with

| Em | C | G | D7 | G |

lots of toys, all for the lit - tle ones Christ - mas joys.

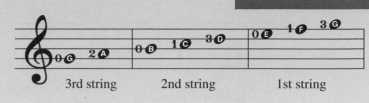

Jingle Bells

James Pierpont

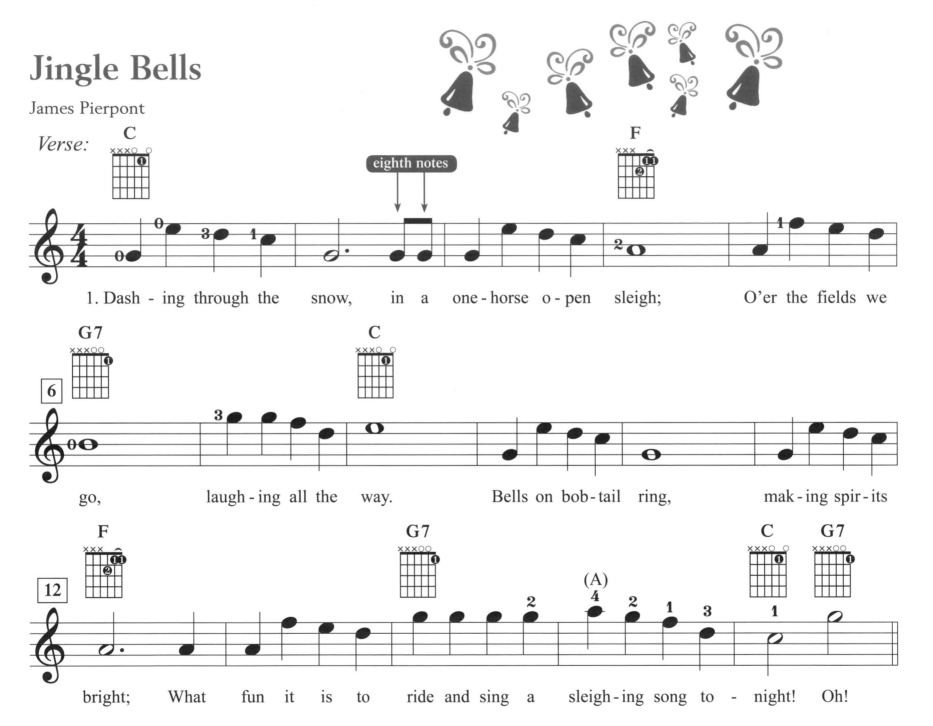

Verse:

1. Dash - ing through the snow, in a one - horse o - pen sleigh; O'er the fields we

go, laugh - ing all the way. Bells on bob - tail ring, mak - ing spir - its

bright; What fun it is to ride and sing a sleigh - ing song to - night! Oh!

MUSIC MASTER

Here is the complete melody of *Jingle Bells*! This version is in the Key of C.
Carefully observe the left-hand fingering indications in measures 14-15. This will prepare
you for a change of position needed to play the note A on the 1st string, 5th fret.

G1065

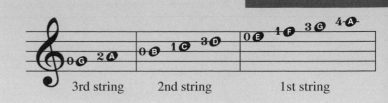

Chorus:

Jin - gle bells, jin - gle bells, jin - gle all the way; Oh, what fun it

is to ride in a one - horse o - pen sleigh. Jin - gle bells, jin - gle bells,

jin - gle all the way; Oh, what fun it is to ride in a one - horse o - pen sleigh! Hey!

Additional Lyrics

2. A day or two ago, I thought I'd take a ride, and soon Miss Fanny Bright, was seated by my side.
The horse was lean and lank, misfortune seemed his lot. We got into a drifted bank and then we got upsot. Oh!
To Chorus:

Chords Used in This Book

The following are complete chord voicings intended to be used by the teacher or a guitarist experienced in chord accompaniment.

The beginning guitarist is encouraged to become familiar with these chord voicings.

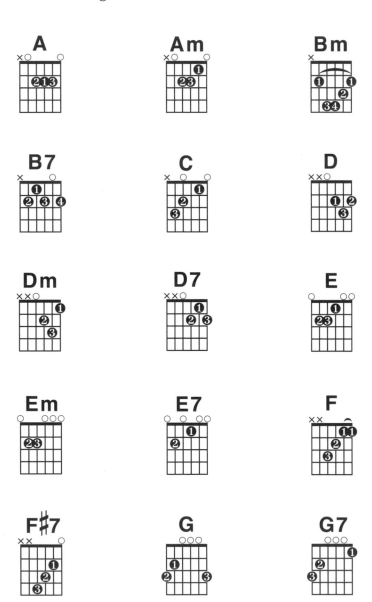

G1065